Hardware Engineer

Hardware engineer

T 29026

Karen Donnelly

the rosen publishing group's
rosen central
new york

I must acknowledge the very generous and enthusiastic response from engineers at Hewlett Packard and Intel. Hewlett Packard's Cathy Lipe, K-12 Education Program Manager, and Dana Houghton, Director of Corporate Affairs, supervised the communication network that made this book possible. Many thanks to these engineers: Intel's Diane Bryant, Debra Cohen, and Ashley Ozawa, and Hewlett Packard's Amy Forsberg, Russ Herrell, Mary Holland, John Hutton, Suzanne Keeler, Ruth McGuffey, Daryl Meekins, Joanne Mistler, Kevin Smith, Roderick Young, and Ted Ziemkowski. Thanks also to everyone else who called with offers to help.

My husband David and my daughters Cathy and Colleen are my best editors. I love you all!

Published in 2000 by The Rosen Publishing Group, Inc.
29 East 21st Street, New York, NY 10010

Copyright © 2000 by The Rosen Publishing Group

First Edition

Library of Congress Cataloging-in-Publication Data

Donnelly, Karen.
　　　Hardware engineer / Karen Donnelly.
　　　　　　p. cm. — (Coolcareers.com)
　　　Includes bibliographical references.
　　　Summary: Discusses what hardware computer engineers do and how to prepare for a career in this field.
　　　ISBN 0-8239-3118-8 (lib. bdg.)
　　　1. Computer science—Vocational guidance Juvenile literature. 2. Computer engineering—Vocational guidance Juvenile literature. [1. Computer science—Vocational guidance. 2. Computer engineering—Vocational guidance 3. Vocational guidance.]   I. Title. II. Series.
　　　QA76.23.D66   2000
　　　621.39'023'73—dc21   99-39173
                                                                          CIP

Manufactured in the United States of America

CONTENTS

ABOUT THIS BOOK

Technology is changing all the time. Just a few years ago, hardly anyone who wasn't a hardcore technogeek had heard of the Internet or the World Wide Web. Computers and modems were way slower and less powerful. If you said "dot com," no one would have any idea what you meant. Hard to imagine, isn't it?

It is also hard to imagine how much more change and growth is possible in the world of technology. People who work in the field are busy imagining, planning, and working toward the future, but even they can't be sure how computers and the Internet will look and function by the time you are ready to start your career. This book is intended to give you an idea of what is out there now so that you can think about what interests you and how to find out more about it.

One thing is clear: Computer-related occupations will continue to increase in number and variety. The demand for qualified workers in these extremely cool fields is increasing all the time. So if you want to get a head start on the competition, or if you just like to fool around with computers, read on!

chapter one

COMPUTERS THEN AND NOW

I like hardware because I can make something that I can hold and play with. It's something that I can take with me and show other people. Hardware is something that can affect the real world.

Ted Ziemkowski
Hardware Designer for Digital Cameras
Hewlett Packard

Look around you. Can you find a computer? If you're in a library or a classroom, that shouldn't be too hard. You probably found a video monitor, a keyboard, a disk drive, and maybe a printer. But what if you were sitting in your living room or riding in a car? Surprisingly, there are computers there, too.

Using the computer in your videocassette recorder, you can set the machine to record a pro-gram weeks in advance. The computerized fuel-injection system in your family's car helps the

Computers help air-traffic controllers keep planes from colliding.

engine to run smoothly. Even the car radio has a computer that allows you to program your favorite stations. Computers keep trains running on schedule and airplanes from colliding. They help us forecast weather and predict earthquakes. They soar into space and explore the depths of the ocean. Computers can even look inside your body!

Every day hardware engineers are designing newer and faster computers and peripheral devices to solve problems that most people have not even dreamed about. As comput-ers control more and more of our world, your chance to play an important role in the field of hardware design grows by leaps and bounds.

It seems that almost every month a manufacturer introduces a newer, faster, smaller computer. Changes occur so quickly that the state-of-the-art machine you buy today could be out-of-date in six months. Like a huge boulder barreling down a hill, computer development began slowly, picked up speed, and now rushes toward the future.

More than 2,000 years ago, the most important ancestor of the modern computer, the abacus, used rows of beads to "store" number values. As early as 1642, mechanical calculators helped people to add, subtract, multiply, and divide. But without electricity, which had not yet been discovered, these primitive calculators had to be operated manually.

In 1890 Herman Hollerith and James Powers worked for the U.S. Census Bureau, the government agency that counts and records how many people live in the United States. They developed machines that could read information punched into cards. The cards were the "memory" of the machine. Companies such as IBM improved these machines, but they were still very slow, typically processing only 50 to 250 cards per minute.

The abacus is an ancestor to the computer.

The first electronic, digital computer was built during World War II by a team of engineers led by J. Presper Eckert and John W. Mauchly. Transistors, integrated circuits, and semiconductors were unknown at the time, so the machine known as ENIAC (Electronic Numerical Integrator and Computer) used 18,000 vacuum tubes. The computer filled an entire room, 30 by 50 feet! It weighed 30 tons and had 100 feet of front panels. It was very expensive to maintain because a vacuum tube is similar to a small lightbulb and easily burns out. ENIAC's separate units were wired together to solve a particular task. When the task or problem changed, the connections and switches had to be reset.

At a public demonstration in 1946, ENIAC was instructed to multiply the number 97,367 by itself 5,000 times. It completed the task in less than half a second, causing a reporter to call

The first electronic computer was built in the late 1940s.

it "faster than thought."
Compared to the
human brain, in which
neurons switch at a
rate of 100 cycles
per second, ENIAC
operated at tens of
thousands of cycles
per second. By the
late 1990s,
tiny silicon
chips called

Computer chips have become considerably smaller over time.

microprocessors, such as the one in Sony's first
PlayStation, would increase to speeds of hundreds of
millions of cycles per second!

This revolution in computer "power," that is, compu-
tational speed, was the work of hardware engineers. They
invented solid-state devices that replaced the vacuum
tubes. They learned how to engrave more and more circuits and switches onto microprocessors. The great
breakthroughs of the software designers—user-friendly
operating systems, complex spreadsheet and word processing programs, and fast-paced animated games—were
possible only after hardware engineers created the

physical components that could handle huge amounts of data quickly. Today a dime-sized microprocessor can make more than 300 million decisions a second, all thanks to the hardware engineer.

chapter two

IF YOU CAN TOUCH IT, IT'S HARDWARE

Hardware is something you can see.
Software is what brings hardware to life.
John Hutton
Research and Development
Engineer, Hewlett Packard

What is the difference between hardware and software? Joanne Mistler, Systems Engineer for Hewlett Packard, made this suggestion: "Think of your body—the muscles and bones—as the 'hardware.' Messages from your brain are the 'software' that controls the hardware."

"Hardware is like a robot that, within limits, does what you tell it to do," said Debra Cohen of Intel. "Software is a language—like English or Chinese—except it's one that both humans and

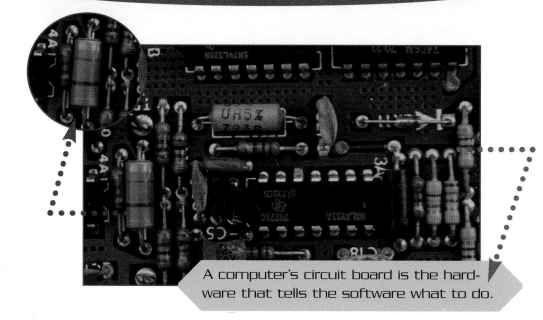

A computer's circuit board is the hardware that tells the software what to do.

computers can understand. We use software to tell hardware what we want it to do."

According to Russ Herrell, Senior Engineer at Hewlett Packard, "Hardware engineers learn how to take complex operations, such as adding two numbers together, and reduce them into a series of simple on/off choices for several electronic switches. Millions of these little switches then get built onto a circuit board or inside an integrated computer chip. Computers aren't smart; they only choose between on and off, but they are very fast, making millions of choices per second."

Computer hardware can be classified according to basic functions. In the broadest scheme of things, these include the input device, the processor and memory storage devices, and the output device.

THE INPUT DEVICE ▶▶▶▶▶▶▶▶▶▶

How do you tell the computer what you want it to do? You "talk" to it using an input device. The most common input device is the computer keyboard. When you push a key, the keyboard sends electrical signals along the cable that connects it to the processor. The signals tell the computer which key you pressed and the computer follows your instructions.

The mouse is an input device, too, designed to make the computer more user-friendly. You don't need to know how to type to use a mouse. You simply roll it over a pad on your desk, and the cursor on the screen moves the same way. When you reach an icon, a picture on the screen that represents the action you want the computer to take, you click a button on the mouse. Almost instantly, the computer will obey your command.

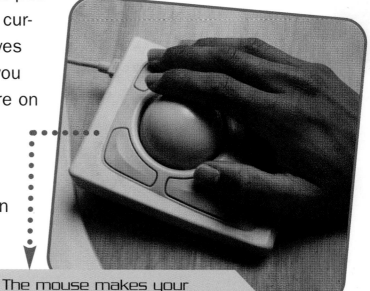

The mouse makes your computer much easier to use.

Light can also send information to your computer. Scanners, fax machines, and digital cameras break down the light from an image or document into tiny segments of black, white, and gray, and then translate these tones into electrical signals.

THE PROCESSOR AND MEMORY STORAGE DEVICES ▶▶▶▶▶▶▶▶▶

Once the signals are sent from the mouse or keyboard, where do they go? A circuit board inside your computer directs them to the central processing unit (CPU), which is the microchip at the heart of your machine. The CPU receives the signals, processes them to perform the instructed task, and sends the results to the output device and the memory storage unit.

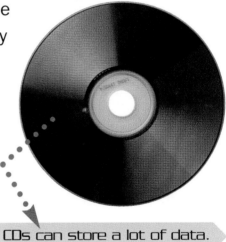

CDs can store a lot of data.

The memory storage unit holds programs, which are the instructions that the computer needs to complete a task, such as word processing. The memory storage unit also holds the data, such as words or numbers, that the computer is instructed to work on. The hard drive inside the computer has a very large storage space. Programs and data can also be stored on floppy disks and CD-ROMs, which can be used to transfer data from one computer to another.

THE OUTPUT DEVICE ▶▶▶▶▶▶▶▶▶▶

Output devices receive signals from the CPU and translate them into images, such as words or numbers, that you can understand. Monitors, printers, fax machines, and even digital alarm clocks are all examples of output devices. Signals from the CPU are sent to them and the images are either printed or displayed. A computer screen uses a million or more red, green, and blue dots in patterns of different brightness to create a color image. Your computer can also produce sound through speakers and headphones.

The monitor is an output device.

Input and output devices, because they have either moving parts or long cable connections to other devices, work slowly compared to CPUs, and it is always a big goal of hardware engineers to improve the speed of input and output devices. Hard drives, too, have moving parts and are relatively slow, and hardware engineers work to increase the storage capacity of fast-access memory devices like RAM (random access memory). The more memory a computer has, the less it will have to "access" its hard drive, and the faster it will work.

chapter three

THE CHIP'S IN CHARGE

Early computers used switches that were the size of a small TV. Now, silicon switches are so small, we can fit 240,000 on the head of a pin.

John Hutton
Research and Development Engineer
Hewlett Packard

In 1999 the average middle-class American household contained about forty microprocessors. They controlled the refrigerator, the smoke alarm, the microwave, and many other devices. That's without a computer. Add a PC and the number increased to fifty microprocessors, controlling the disk drive, the video display, and so on. A typical family car may use as many as twenty chips to control the radio, the air bag, remote door locks, and dash-board displays.

So what is a microchip and how does it work? It's a small piece of a mineral called silicon, usually no bigger than a postage stamp. The material itself is worth less than a penny. But it's what's engraved on the chip that gives it power.

In most towns, there are pipes that carry water to the various buildings, regulated by valves that turn the flow of water on and off. In the same way, there are "pipes" and "valves" engraved into the microchip that control the flow of electric current and direct it to do useful work. A chip designer figures out the most efficient pathways and switches to make the chip perform various tasks as quickly as possible.

Generally a smaller size makes one chip faster than another.

Tiny microchips allow the fast processing of all kinds of information.

It would take you only seconds to walk across a room, but much longer to cross a large park. On a smaller chip, the electricity doesn't have to travel as far. But hardware engineers also have to cram as many electrical pathways as they can onto each chip so that the chip can handle more tasks and hold more data. Engraving more and more electrical pathways as the size of the microprocessor shrinks is the great challenge facing hardware engineers.

The power of microprocessors is measured by their speed. Speed is measured by how many millions of switching operations, or cycles, per second a chip can handle. One million cycles per second is known as one megahertz (MHz), named for German scientist Heinrich Hertz. In just the last few years, chip speeds have increased from 50 to 75 MHz to as much as 300 MHz or more. To put this in perspective, a 300 MHz microprocessor can read through a program containing 5 million lines of code or a database of 5 million numbers sixty times in one second! And the quest for even faster chips continues.

chapter four

LEARNING MATH AND SCIENCE

A love of math and science and the thrill of conquering the unknown are essential ingredients to being a good engineer.

Diane Bryant
Engineering Manager
Intel

Mathematics is the language that computers understand. Engineers can explain how an electronic circuit works using mathematical equations. They can then use these equations to figure out how to improve the circuit. If you are interested in becoming a hardware engineer, a strong interest in science and mathematics is important.

"If you like math, then you probably like to understand dimensions and calculations that help describe how different things work," said Joanne Mistler. "Some hardware engineers focus on how to fit their designs into the tiny spaces of a handheld computer game or a cellular phone. Other hardware engineers have to figure out the mathematical equations that will allow these devices to work."

Some hardware designers create new computer games.

"I used to be fascinated by suspension bridges and wondered how people could figure out how to set them up so that they wouldn't fall," Joanne continued. "My eighth-grade science teacher talked about forces and showed me why water would stay in a bucket as he swung it around in a circle. That got me interested in physics, even though, at the time, I had no idea what physics was!"

A scientific approach to sports and music led John Hutton, Research and Development Engineer at Hewlett Packard, to his interest in engineering. He wanted to know how things work. "How can I kick the soccer ball farther?" John asked. "I drew pictures of my leg and the ball. I thought about how my foot would hit the ball." In basketball, he wondered at what angle he should shoot the ball to make a basket. Too high, and his aim would be off. Too low, and he would hit the rim. He played the saxophone and wondered how pushing different keys changed the note he was playing. "How did the air I was blowing make the noise in the first place? How did the noise travel to my ear, and how did my ear work?"

"Keep your options open!" Debra Cohen added. "Don't limit yourself by opting out of math and science classes. You can always change your mind later and do something that's not technology-related for a career. But if you opt out of college-prep math and science classes in junior high or high school, you'll have a hard time later on if you decide you want to get involved in engineering."

COMPUTER CAMP ▶▶▶▶▶▶▶▶▶

Computer camps can be a great way to learn how computers work while you make new friends and have fun. Most activities at computer camp center around programming, but understanding programs can be a big help to someone interested in designing the hardware to run them.

In 1977 Dr. Michael Zabinski founded National Computer Camps, America's first camps devoted to teaching kids about computers. "At computer camp, kids learn to think in a way that's different from the usual way of thinking," said Dr. Zabinski. "They learn to organize their thoughts step by step and to break down tasks into simple sequences. Like putting on your socks before your shoes—input, then processing, then output. They learn to understand how the computer handles instructions. Hardware design requires logic and understanding of how data is stored and processed. Hardware design is the architecture."

To be a hardware designer, you must possess a logical mind.

At computer camp, kids also get a chance to take computers apart to see what's inside. "We do this in two ways," explained Dr. Zabinski. "First, kids can carefully take apart new computers with an instructor." The instructor actually takes the computer apart, but the kids get to look inside and see what's there. The instructor explains what all the parts are and how they work. Kids learn about maintenance—about how you replace your hard drive, for example. They can watch the platters of the hard drive spin." Kids are also given older, out-of-date computers to take apart themselves. "The old computers are structurally the same," said Dr. Zabinski, "just not as fast."

chapter five

WHAT DO YOU DO ALL DAY?

Every job will teach you something new.

Ted Ziemkowski

The best way to find out what hardware engineers do is to ask them! These engineers from Intel and Hewlett Packard have very different jobs, but all of them are hardware engineers. What do they do all day? They'll tell you!

RODERICK YOUNG, ENGINEER ▶▶▶▶▶▶▶▶▶▶▶▶▶

"I'm a chip designer by trade. That means that a team of us will work for months, maybe a year, on a project, and the result is a little piece of silicon no bigger than your thumbnail. But that little chip could be the brains of the next computer!

"When I started, almost twenty years ago, we used to do a design by actually drawing the internals of a chip by hand. A large crew of people would check that everything was right. The whole thing might take two years, and you were lucky if anything on your chip worked the first time. Today one designer with the right software can sit down at a PC and finish one simple chip in a few days. And it usually works."

ASHLEY OZAWA, CIRCUIT DESIGNER ▶▶▶▶▶▶▶▶▶▶

"I design microprocessors. They take input, process instructions, and determine an output. I design the circuitry that lets electrical signals flow through the microprocessor while it follows instructions. I also have to test my designs to make sure that they work correctly."

Microprocessors receive and process complicated data.

TED ZIEMKOWSKI, HARDWARE DESIGNER▸▸▸▸▸▸▸▸▸▸

"I am now a hardware designer for digital cameras. I love it! I really like talking to customers and understanding what they want. And, since I am a digital camera fan, I am one of my best customers. The better camera I make, the better toy I will have when I am done.

"It took me a while to get to this point. I started out doing many interesting things, but not exactly what I wanted to do. The most important thing I did was to learn from every experience."

JOHN HUTTON, RESEARCH AND DEVELOPMENT ENGINEER ▸▸

"I make computer chips. To make a CPU, we go through many steps. First, we imagine what we would like our chip to do. Then we use math and science to plan how it might work. Our final design uses a special computer language called binary. Our entire chip is made of transistors, which are very small, brainlike cells that "talk" binary. We divide the chip into chunks and start figuring out where each tiny transistor will go. This is quite a job, since millions of transistors live together on the same chip."

DEBRA COHEN, PROJECT MANAGER ►►►►►►►►

"I've worked at Intel for ten years. During that time, I've had many jobs. For the first three years, I was an applications engineer, helping other engineers understand how to use Intel computer chips. Then I spent a couple of years as a validation engineer, making sure that the chips we designed worked properly. After that I worked on designing the chips themselves. After a few years, I became a team leader,

Project managers oversee the work of other engineers.

supervising up to four other design engineers. Recently, I've moved into a project management position. I'm responsible for ensuring that all the various teams involved in designing, manufacturing, testing, and selling our products have the tools that they need to get the job done right."

AMY FORSBERG, PROGRAM MANAGER ▸▸▸▸▸▸▸▸▸

"Right out of college, I worked on part of a computer chip. From there I had a number of jobs that revolved around the design of the hardware for a new computer. With each new job, I was given more responsibility for ensuring that more of the hardware worked correctly. Today I do program management. Like the orchestra conductor, I make sure that all the different people working on developing a new computer, including the hardware designers, programmers, manufacturers, marketers, and support, do their tasks at the right time."

DIANE BRYANT, ENGINEERING MANAGER ▸▸▸▸▸▸▸▸

"Fourteen years ago, my first year at Intel was spent designing a hard disk controller. This hardware gives the computer access to the data on the hard drive. Next I was part of a large team of engineers that designed microprocessors for notebook computers. Then I became a manager, coordinating teams of engineers to design hardware for notebooks. Now I coordinate a team of engineers designing a microprocessor for very fast computers that support the Internet."

KEVIN SMITH, TEST ENGINEER ▶▶

"As a test engineer, I try to break things! When I was a child, I got in trouble for doing this. Now I get paid for it! I take computers, beat them up, find out how they fail, and then recommend redesigns. I asked my eight-year-old son if he remembered his toy airplane. It broke the first day that he played with it. My job testing computers would be like testing that toy. I would find out how kids play with a toy, figure out how to simulate that play in the test lab, and then test it. If the toy did break, I would help to find out how it broke and recommend a way to make the design better. Then children would not be disappointed.

"I put computers on a vibration table and shake them. I drop them to the floor from twelve feet up. I heat them and cool them. It is always interesting to see how things break and how we can make machines stronger."

chapter six

BE A
TEAM PLAYER

Teams are a fact of life. It is good to be a leader, but just as important to be a contributor so your team is the leader, not just you.

Suzanne Keeler
Packaging Engineer, Hewlett Packard

Designing a computer can be a very complicated task. Many engineers with different jobs must work together to build one. Ruth McGuffey, a project manager at Hewlett Packard, said, "Engineers are often portrayed as nerdy outcasts, sitting in a small room somewhere inventing things by themselves. That's not the case. Teams of hardware engineers create computers. Each member is responsible for a particular piece."

"There's nothing like the feeling of working together as a team," said Roderick Young. "When you get the right team together, you can accomplish far more than you ever imagined." John Hutton added, "What does one plus one equal? Two? In math, of course. But when you're talking about teamwork, one plus one equals three or four. Two people working together are powerful. They can do much more than each person working alone. When you sit down with other engineers and start working, you come up with great ideas."

In school you often work on your own. You are expected to do your own homework, and you are not expected to share your test answers with anyone else. This is because your teachers want to evaluate your individual knowledge and skills. In business, it's a little different.

Working in teams can greatly improve the quality of ideas.

Because building something like a new computer can be

very expensive, it is much more important to do things right than to prove that one person can do it all. It's sometimes hard to see our own mistakes, and the members of a team can correct each other's errors. The team concept has become very popular in all sorts of businesses. In a complex field like computer development, teamwork is indispensable.

Working on group projects at school will prepare you for teamwork.

Playing on sports teams, performing with an orchestra, or working on group projects can help prepare you for teamwork. "Throughout my schooling, from fourth grade through high school, I was a member of the band," said Diane Bryant. "A band is a sum of many individual instruments, playing in a synchronized manner. Being part of a band taught me the need to commit and perform my best, to allow all the band members to collectively achieve our goals."

In an industry where everything changes very quickly, teamwork can be the key to staying ahead. "Since everything is moving so fast, we need to use teams to get a lot of work done in a short amount of time," said Ted Ziemkowski. "A design that would take one person one year to finish might take a team of four to six people only three months."

"Working in a team is so important," said Suzanne Keeler. "If you are a piece of a puzzle, you will make the best decision for your piece. But what happens when you have to put it all together? Wouldn't it be nice to see the whole picture ahead of time? That's what working in a team does. It lets you see the whole picture from different angles and with different pieces already in place."

chapter seven

BEYOND HIGH SCHOOL

If you want something rewarding like a career in engineering, you have to be willing to put your mind to it and then back up your decision with actions.

Debra Cohen
Project Manager, Intel

How do you actually learn to be a hardware engineer? Obviously you will need technical training. But there's no need to specialize right away. "Your education should be an exploration, a time to try new challenges," said Russ Herrell. "Don't be fooled into thinking that people know all about their engineering careers before they actually get to work."

Debra Cohen began by majoring in biochemistry. She eventually decided not to pursue a career in chemistry, but she was grateful for all the math and physics courses she had taken. "I love unraveling mysteries," she said. "And the world of electrons, transistors, and circuits was just that!"

Suzanne Keeler suggested going to a large college or university with many departments and lots of opportunities. "There are so many unusual and wonderful majors to choose from," she said. "Talk to upperclassmen and explore different majors. Other great computer-related majors are supply chain manage- ment, materials logistics man- agement,

Most universities offer computer-related courses and majors.

mechanical engineering, and technical marketing."

In addition to classroom courses, you can gain further experience by participating in a work-study or internship program. While studying at Northeastern University in Boston, Joanne Mistler participated in such a program at

Raytheon. She began by writing software simulations for missiles and then worked in the testing of microwave equipment. She even had her own design project for a missile guidance receiver. "This experience was tremendous," Joanne said. "When I graduated, I already knew what to expect and had a good idea what I liked. Also, Raytheon already knew me and knew my capabilities." As a result, Raytheon sponsored her graduate studies with a full scholarship to Tufts University in Boston.

Ted Ziemkowski believes that his college professors and his internship at IBM were a "killer combination." He learned electrical engineering from two different perspectives. "If I had a problem understanding the professor, I could ask my mentors," he said. "Their answers usually approached the problem from an angle that was more practical and easier for me to understand."

An internship will also allow you to work safely on real projects. You will probably be given independent assignments, like most other employees. But your mentor will check your work and can help you correct any mistakes you make. During her internship at Cadence Design Systems, Ashley Ozawa learned how to do the physical design, or layout, of a circuit before she learned it at school. "The layout that I did in my internship was much more difficult than any project that I had to do in school," she said.

Internships can also help you figure out what engineering career to choose. "I was able to experience both manufacturing and design in my internships," said Ashley. "I was able to decide what I like and what I didn't like. In school there is no opportunity to experience manufacturing in a factory-like setting. There is no

Internships are a great way to get your start in the field.

opportunity to work on large-scale, long-term design projects." Her internship projects helped her to decide that she enjoyed design work more than manufacturing. So she chose a job as a hardware designer.

After graduation, Ted Ziemkowski's experience in his internship helped him to make the right job choice. "Without the internship, I think I might have just picked any job," he said. "I would have wasted a lot of time learning that it was not the right job for me."

Finally, while taking science and math courses and working on your internship, don't neglect English! "The only difference between a $30-an-hour engineer and a $40-an-hour engineer is that one of them can write well," said Roderick Young. "The way to learn to write well is to read a lot. It's not that painful; just find something you like."

chapter eight

THE FUTURE IS NOW

Enjoy the challenge of change.

Russ Herrell

Hewlett Packard

Computers are constantly changing. A hardware engineer must be able to see the problems of the future and develop solutions today. "Next year in school, you will have harder subjects and more work," said John Hutton. "With computers, the same thing is true. Next year computers will have to do more work than this year. Engineers have to keep learning, just like you do in school."

What should you do to prepare for a career as a hardware engineer? "The best thing you can do is learn as much as you can," said John Hutton. "If you are curious about something, ask questions about it. Try to figure out how things work. Let your mind lead you."

"Always do your best, study hard, and look for new paths to travel down," advised Suzanne Keeler. "People are not 'lucky' in the job or the grades they get. People work hard."

Always do your best, work hard, and keep your options open.

"Don't be afraid to take hard classes! There's not much you can't do if you set your mind to it," said Debra Cohen. "That doesn't mean somebody's going to hand you what you need to know. You're going to have to work for it. But don't let that stop you."

And finally, Ted Ziemkowski said, "It's a blast, and it pays well! There is nothing better than getting paid for doing something you love."

WORDS.COM: GLOSSARY

central processing unit (CPU) The microchip inside the computer that actually makes calculations and processes data.

hardware The physical parts of a computer that you can actually touch.

input device The parts of a computer that let you send signals to the central processing unit, which allow you to tell it what to do. Input devices include the keyboard, mouse, and scanner.

memory storage unit A device that can hold data and programs in digital format, such as a hard drive, floppy disks, or CD-ROMs.

output device A device such as a printer or monitor that receives data from the central processing unit and converts it into images, words, or numbers.

silicon A chemical element that engineers use to make semiconductors, so that the flow of electricity can be controlled like a switch.

software Software consists of the coded instructions that tell computers what to do. Software is stored on pieces of hardware, like hard drives and CD-ROMs, but the software itself exists only as a series of electromagnetic fields.

RESOURCES.COM: WEB SITES

Ada Project
http://www.cs.yale.edu/~tap/tap.html
Sponsored by Yale University. Information specifically designed to inform and attract women and girls. Includes the Role Model Project aimed at inspiring girls age nine to sixteen to choose computer careers.

American Computer Science League
http://www.acsl.org
Organizes computer science contests and computer programming contests for junior and senior high school students.

Computer Clubhouse
http://www.computerclubhouse.org
An after-school learning environment where young people can explore their own interests and become confident learners through the use of technology.

Computer Museum
http://www.tcm.org
Sponsored by the Boston Computer Museum. Includes interactive exhibits and computer history.

Future Engineers
http://www.futureengineers.com
Advice and tips for students from other students and professional engineers. Sponsored by Hewlett Packard.

Future Scientists and Engineers of America
http://www.fsea.org
A nonprofit organization that promotes science and engineering among American youth in grades four through twelve.

Hewlett Packard E-Mail Mentoring Program
http://www.telementor.org/hp/.
Hewlett Packard's e-mail mentors encourage students to study science and math. The program will provide over 3,000 mentors to fifth- through twelfth-grade students, and teachers who are integrating e-mail mentoring into their science and math curriculum.

Junior Summit
http://www.jrsummit.net
MIT's Media Lab connects kids around the world through the Junior Summit.

National Computer Camps
http://www.corpcenter.com/ncc/
Information about America's first computer camp, directed by Dr. Michael Zabinski. Information is also available from P.O. Box 585, Orange, CT 06477.

Public Broadcasting Service
http://www.pbs.org/technology
An ever-changing source of up-to-date technology information. Includes interactive games and puzzles and teacher resources.

BOOKS.COM:
FOR FURTHER READING

Cook, Peter, Scott Manning, and Ed Murrow. *Why Doesn't My Floppy Disk Flop? And Other Kids Computer Questions Answered by the Compududes.* New York: John Wiley and Sons, 1999.

Pabst, Thomas. *Tom's Hardware Guide.* Indianapolis: Que Books, 1998.

Barbarello, James. *PC Hardware Projects.* Indianapolis: Prompt Publishers, 1998.

Keenan, Douglas. *Introduction to Computer Hardware Theory, Maintenance, Troubleshooting.* Denton, TX: RonJon Publishing, 1998.

Macauley, David. *The New Way Things Work.* Boston: Houghton Mifflin, 1998.

Reeves, Diane Lindsay and Peter Kent. *Career Ideas for Kids Who Like Computers.* New York: Facts on File Publications, 1998.

INDEX

48

About the Author
Karen Donnelly is a freelance writer of nonfiction books for children. She lives in Bethany, Connecticut, with her husband and two daughters.

Photo Credits
Cover photo by Thaddeus Harden; p. 8 Reuters/Photographer Unknown/ Archive; pp. 9, 12 Archive; pp. 13, 21, 23, 36, 38, 41 by Thaddeus Harden; p. 18 CORBIS/Charles O'Rear; p. CORBIS/Owen Franken; p. 28 © David Strover; p. 32 @ SUPER-STOCK; p. 33 © Steve Skjold.

Design and Layout
Annie O'Donnell

Consulting Editor
Amy Haugesag